Connect The Dots
Strategies and Meditations On Self-Education

By Paul Jun

Copyright 2014 Paul Jun. All rights reserved.

ISBN-13: 978-1495245084
ISBN-10: 149524508X

If you wish to use any quotes or passages, please do so as long as you give credit where it's due.

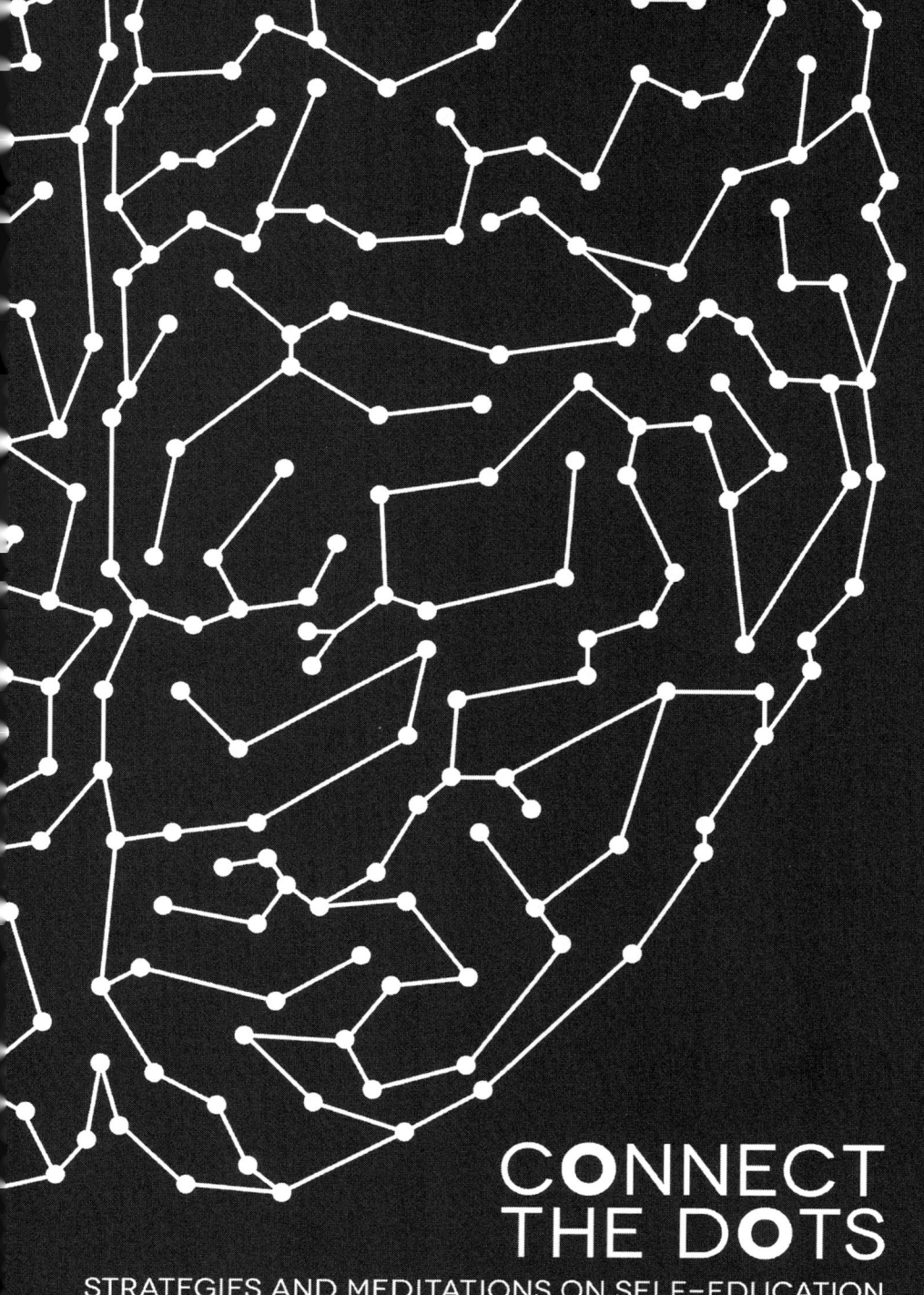

CONNECT THE DOTS
STRATEGIES AND MEDITATIONS ON SELF-EDUCATION

PAUL JUN

Table of Contents

What This Book Isn't About 2
What This Book *Is* About 6
Every Successful Person That Came Before You Would
    Be Jealous of You. 14
Reading 18
"Put your pens down and listen!" 34
Building An Engine of Knowledge 40
Consciously Curating Your Channels. 46
The Commonplace Book 52
Don't Just Absorb But Also Apply 58
Connect Your Dots. 62
Resources. 70
Notes and Further Reading 80
Acknowledgements 84

"The most important knowledge is that which guides the way you lead your life." — Seneca

What This Book Isn't About

This book isn't about putting an x-ray over the current education system and relentlessly tapping on the black shadowy cancer blob. I'm not here to point out the myriad flaws and failed expectations, the problems with the system at large. I am not the lone critic, no doubt about that, but that would make for a much longer book.

After graduating high school and immediately entering community college, I felt lost. I was neither creatively nor intellectually stimulated and had totally checked out. As a result, I was failing most of my classes. Like many of my peers, I had no idea what I wanted to do with my life. And as clarity continuously eluded me, I felt more and more like a grunt in a factory.

I hated it.

On a whim, I created a website and started writing about the video games I was playing. It was a great outlet for me and I was good at it. Though, sadly, I would never get paid to play video games all day, I had uncovered a skill that I could develop. More than that, I had unwittingly stumbled onto a potential career path: I could be a writer.

I began studying a multitude of writers, bloggers, and entrepreneurs — people who were leveraging the Internet and all its tools to build an audience and share their ideas. My own ideas floated around like dots in my mind but I was failing to connect them. *Is writing what it was years ago? How are people doing this?*

After months of studying writing, online sharing, and Internet commerce, I realized that I was *learning*. I was exploring topics, weighing data and opinions, and reaching my own understanding. I was being challenged —better still, I was challenging myself — and taking initiative in my own education. With each new writer that interested me, I threw myself down a rabbit hole of interviews, articles, and, of course, every one of their books. I would ask myself, "Why does this writer have an audience? What is it that they do? What value do they provide? What are the patterns here? How are they making a living?" Eventually the question became, "why not me?"

It took me years to realize that I had adapted to the mediocrity of industrial education. In essence, assuming control over my own education and studying the subjects that were practical for my goals felt very natural. I was learning on my own *and* having fun. I was no longer dependent on a classroom or a teacher to exercise my mind. My education and personal development were now internally motivated and measured by tangible improvement, and that is far more compelling than "A, B, C, D, or F".

"Devotion to the truth is the hallmark of morality; there is no greater, nobler, more heroic form of devotion than the act of a man who assumes the responsibility of thinking." — Ayn Rand

What This Book *Is* About

Once I embraced my craft — once I mustered the courage to tell my parents and friends, "I'm going to be a writer" — my bank statements became flooded with book purchases. I *loved* learning through reading and tirelessly churned through pages. I started writing about what I read. My blog became "a record of my own learning,"[1] a manifestation of my self-education.

As Seneca once said, *"You can't imagine how much of an alteration I see each day bringing about in me. 'Send me, too' you will be saying, 'the things you found so effectual.' Indeed I desire to transfer every one of them to you; part of joy in learning is that it puts me in a position to teach; nothing, however outstanding and however helpful, will ever give me any pleasure if the knowledge is to be for my benefit alone. If wisdom were offered me on the one condition that I should keep it shut away and not divulge it to anyone, I should reject it. There is no enjoying the possession of anything valuable unless one has someone to share it with."*

Self-education is a skill that I've honed over the last few years. It has become a wellspring of self-awareness, humility, motivation, understanding, purpose, and joy. Being able to solve a problem, or at least

---

1 A phrase borrowed from Maria Popova.

What This Book Is About

see it in a new light, is the result of connecting the many dots that you accumulate throughout your studies.

What do I mean by "connecting the dots"?

A "dot" can be anything, really: a new thought, an idea, a question, anything that captures your attention. A dot is also your personal experience, what you do know, and what you love. "Connecting the dots" is just that: making connections, stringing together different ideas and information to form a larger picture, a deeper understanding, a new awareness. It is the process by which you learn and each thing you learn along the way.

The concept is as simple as the puzzles you did when you were a kid. At first glance, you're simply staring at a mess of numbered dots. It's nearly impossible to guess what the picture could be. But, by slowly connecting the dots, the image emerges. Dot after dot, it becomes more evident. Specks on a page become a picture that has meaning.

The more you diversify the dots you obtain and connect, the deeper your understanding becomes. The more diverse your understanding, the more your knowledge base expands. Cross-pollinate different ideas. Be open-minded. Consider evidence and perspectives that challenge your beliefs. As you try to make sense of something new, your brain will connect the dots you already have to help you understand. What picture does it create? What is missing? What new information—new dots—will fill those gaps and create a clearer picture?

Like anything worthwhile, connecting the dots is a muscle that needs exercise in order to develop and grow. Reading a Wikipedia page on a subject may provide a rudimentary foundation of knowledge but I'm not here to talk to about how to dominate at pub trivia. Facts have their place, of course, but this book is about *building understanding* through self-education.

By leveraging the multitude of resources that facilitate self-education, you can collect and converge an assortment of dots that have possible potential for connection. Then take it a step further. Engage with with what you learn. Think deeply. Write about it. Experiment. Discuss it with your peers. All of this will strengthen the connections you make. It will expand your knowledge base, deepen your understanding, and generate even more curiosity. As you connect the dots, you become aware of how much or how little you know about the subject. If you feel frustrated, that's okay, treat it as your cue to dig deeper. If things are making sense, it doesn't mean that you've mastered the subject, but rather the connections are being made and the potential for deeper connections are possible.

This book isn't about learning how to speed read or memorize stuff better. I'm not providing hacks; I'm helping you create a new mindset. **I want to help you reframe what education means to you.** Are you actively pursuing knowledge? Is learning as important to you as breathing or eating, or is it something that you're forced to do? Are you allowing your mind to explore different subjects? Are you cross-pollinating ideas and reaching new insights? What do you think about all day long? The first transformation of the mind is realizing that education is not a place or a deadline. It's not the attainment of a degree or the following of a syllabus. It's a practice, a habit, a part of your daily diet.

At 24, I've self-published two books, worked on projects with people I've met online, created a digital and print manifesto that has been shared

What This Book Is About

many times, and my articles have been read by thousands of people on a multitude of sites. I've delved into subjects that are way out of my comfort zone, exploring philosophy, psychology, marketing, neuroscience, entrepreneurship, art, culture, and design. Reflecting on my path thus far, I realize that this is the kind of education I want for my whole life. Learning challenges and changes your worldview, enhances your craft by exposing you to different ideas, and transforms you on every level: how you think, feel, and behave.

I define learning as *the acquisition and manipulation of information not only gained through maturation but through relentlessly exploring the unknown and connecting the dots.*

In the words of Sir Ken Robinson, author of *Out of Our Minds: Learning to Be Creative*, a must-read to understand the birth of our mass education system [emphasis by me]: *"Creative insights often occur by making unusual connections: seeing analogies between ideas that have not previously been related. All of our existing ideas have creative possibilities. Creative insights occur when they are combined in unexpected ways or applied to questions or issues with which they are not normally associated. Arthur Koestler describes this as a process of bi-association: when we bring together ideas from different areas that are not normally connected,* **so that we think not on one plane as in routine linear thinking but on several planes at once.** *Creative thought involves breaching the boundaries between different frames of reference."*

As Sugatra Mitra said in his inspiring TEDTalk of 2013, *"It's not about making learning happen, it's about letting learning happen."* The way a yogi practices compassion on and off their mat, are you allowing learning to be as vital as drinking water in your everyday routine? Today, access to learning material is readily available and unremittingly expanding.

Connect The Dots

It can be completely overwhelming and the abundance of choices can easily lead to no choice at all.

I want to help you foster a desire to learn. Make it a priority and actively pursue it in a disciplined way. Be aware of the opportunity available to you right now, and realize that the efforts you put into reshaping your mind affects the quality of your life.

On top of reading over a 100 books a year, I have fallen in love with podcasts, listen to at least 10 interviews a week, watch many educational videos like TEDTalks, and my blog feed consistently stimulates my mind and exposes me to new perspectives and ideas. I've taken a few online courses that offer lifelong access to the community. I've emailed thought leaders and masters and received honest feedback and advice. I've turned my Twitter from a collection of rant-filled regurgitated opinions and negativity into a wisdom machine by following brilliant leaders, writers, entrepreneurs, artists, scientists, and journalists.

This is the education I wish I could have had years ago.

This is revolutionary. Even a decade ago none of this would have been possible. For thousands of years access to information was locked away by the elite and privileged. Systems, or a lack thereof, hindered the common man from enriching his mind. Now, the gates aren't just open, they're blown off the hinges, and anyone with a desire to learn can be exposed to mentors and teachers that nourish an enlightening experience.

In the words of Austin Kleon, author of *Steal Like An Artist*, "It's one of my theories that when people give you advice, they're really just talking to themselves in the past. This book is me talking to a previous version of myself."

What This Book Is About

My goal is the same. I'm writing this book to my old self, encouraging him to stop *waiting* for something to happen. *Waiting* to learn and practice the necessary skills to lead the career and life I desire. *Waiting* to be self-aware. *Waiting* to be motivated. *Waiting* to contribute. *Waiting* to create. *Waiting* to be picked. *Waiting* to understand why things are they way they are, and what I can possibly do to make a difference.

There's no saying when the education system will change. Nor can there be any certainty that change, if it ever does come, will bring a solution for you. I believe that taking the initiative of educating yourself is the best way to reconnect with a love of learning that has perhaps been lost after years in a classroom. I hope it provides a sense of urgency, a realization that there is so much out there that can benefit your life and your work.

Self-education is a timeless asset, a skill that requires discipline and patience but will ultimately provide the key to a great life. Learning is an integral part of being a human being, and to ignore it, or worse, to wait for it to happen, is an exercise in self-sabotage.

"Louis C.K. has famously proven that he doesn't need the tyranny of the booker — he booked himself. Marc Maron didn't wait to be cast on Saturday Night Live — he started his own podcast and earned a million listeners. Our cultural instinct is to wait to get picked. To seek out the permission, authority, and safety that come from a publisher or a talk-show host or even a blogger who says, 'I pick you.' Once you reject that impulse and realize that no one is going to select you — that Prince Charming has chosen another house in his search for Cinderella — then you can actually get to work. The myth that the CEO is going to discover you and nurture you and ask you to join her for lunch is just that, a Hollywood myth. Once you understand that there are problems waiting to be solved, once you realize that you have all the tools and all the mission you need, then opportunities to contribute abound." — Seth Godin

Every Successful Person That Came Before You Would Be Jealous of You

In 1848, the California Gold Rush captivated the world as gold-seekers arrived from all over to carve out their stake. California was a new frontier, free of so many of the established boundaries that existed in the eastern side of the country. The West offered a truly open opportunity to anyone that could get himself there. Many arrived with little and walked away with a fortune.

The digital revolution offers a new gem. I view the Internet as an ever-growing mountain: you can choose an area, grab a pickaxe, mine the minerals, and craft the tools that are favorable to your endeavors. Simply put, you can learn *anything*, connect with anyone, and create things that people want.

The diverse channels that champion self-education are readily available and are expanding by the day. As Robert Greene says in his book, *Mastery*: "Millions of people who were not part of the right social class, gender, and ethnic group were rigidly excluded from the possibility of pursuing their calling. Even if people wanted to follow their inclinations, access to the information and knowledge pertaining to that particular field was controlled by elites.

Every Successful Person That Came Before You Would Be Jealous of You

That is why there are relatively few Masters in the past and why they stand out so much." There are many modern masters that we can learn from today, and there isn't a doubt in my mind that they learned from the masters in the past.

Einstein Would Trade Places With You

Right now, the opportunity to explore **any** subject and learn **anything** abounds. If you want to learn coding, it's available in a multitude of formats and styles and classes. If you want to write, go ahead and start a blog for free. If you want to finally learn to draw, you can watch YouTube tutorials, follow artists on Instagram, and take online courses (I took one for $20 on a site called Skillshare). There are no gatekeepers locking away secret information. Nothing is stopping you from taking your expertise and understanding to the next level.

You can organize your own study groups through an online community, social media, or a service like Krypton Community College created by Seth Godin. You have access to Ivy League courses through Coursera or edX, if you want to feel fancy. You can create your own syllabus. You can read a biography and realize that the author faced similar problems as you did and overcame them. You can read books that contain life-altering perspectives and ideas, that provide motivation, understanding, and wisdom — some for as little as a penny. You can listen to an interview with an expert in your industry and profit off their experiences. You can listen to podcasts about any topic you can imagine. You can follow all the brilliant people in the world, assuming they use the same social network as you. All for free.

Are you listening? *You can learn anything you want.*

Connect The Dots

No one is hiding anything from you. You have access to the same information as an Ivy League student, a CEO of a major company, or the Dalai Lama.

The reason most people don't recognize this as an opportunity is because they lack a desire to educate themselves — they don't see it as fun or important ... or maybe they don't know how. The challenge is learning how to think for yourself — taking opinions, research, history, and facts and swishing it around your head to arrive at an understanding. It's far easier to have someone instill fear into you to do something — because, hey, if you don't score high on this test you won't graduate, and if you don't graduate you won't get a job and you'll die! The path of self-education enforces and cultivates self-awareness. It puts you in a position to think very deeply.

There is a crucial difference between today's self-educational opportunities and the Gold Rush: California's mines were tapped out in less than a decade. It's only going to get better and easier from here. More and more services will be created that champion the idea of self-education, of providing information in a structured and beautiful way to stimulate and feed hungry minds. The only challenge is **starting**.

"There is a time in every man's education when he arrives at the conviction that envy is ignorance; that imitation is suicide; that he must take himself for better, for worse, as his portion; that though the wide universe is full of good, no kernel of nourishing corn can come to him but through his toil bestowed on that plot of ground which is given to him to till. The power which resides in him is new in nature, and none but he knows what that is which he can do, nor does he know until he has tried."

— Ralph Waldo Emerson

Reading

Reading is undoubtedly my favorite way to learn. I wish I had been doing it for all my life. When I learn about the habits of successful men and women, the shared trait that I consistently see is that they are voracious readers. In turn, their understanding of the world and everything in it is far greater than most. It is both humbling and motivating to embrace someone else's perspective and there's no better access than books. I am where I am in life because of the amount of books I've read, and my gratitude is so great that I felt compelled to make the first focus of this book: *reading*.

When I first embarked on the path of self-education, I began with reading. And nearly dozed off ten pages in. My eyes got heavy, my mind wandered, and I couldn't tell you what I read even two minutes later. I remember the first book that I picked up — a random, dusty victim in my closet — was *The Great Gatsby*. I think I had it because of my high school's summer reading list. It took me 8 months to finish it, and even then I had no idea what it was about. All I knew was that the 20's fascinated me, and Daisy had to get her shit straight.

I can understand how difficult reading is; it's like starting your diet, *again*. Successful men and women have implored their audience in interviews and commencement speeches and in their own books to start reading, yet few heed their counsel.

Reading

Reading is probably the most important thing you can be doing right now. But, as with anything else worth doing, it requires focus and consistent effort. Below, I outline the strategy I used to go from never reading a book to devouring over 100 books a year on a multitude of subjects.

1. Create the desire

Well the first thing I'd ask you is, why do you want to read?

Is it to escape? To learn? Purpose begets motivation. To suddenly pick up a book because your boss told you so isn't going to work in the long run. My purpose was to learn. I kept telling myself that the more knowledgeable I became, the better chance I had to pull myself out of my rut (nobody wants to be a lost college student, always angry, or jobless). It was better than playing video games. Now, after reading so many books in the past years, I can confidently say that books helped me become a better person. Reading transformed me: my thinking, my desires, and my worldview.

Don't wait around for the desire to strike. Most people don't read and won't ever, even if their heroes are begging to them to do so.

You have to constantly tell yourself a story about how this will benefit you as a human being. Admitting that there are a lot of smart people out there — much smarter than you — *compelled* to share valuable knowledge learned through their life experiences may be a good start. People have been writing about the same problems for hundreds, if not thousands of years, all providing different solutions and perspectives. Simply put, what you're going through right now has a solution in a book somewhere. When I saw the connection between people who lead extraordinary lives to the amount of books they read — the understanding that they possess due to constantly expanding their minds — how could I say no? This was my golden ticket to a better life. Was it easy to start? No. But it was better than the alternative.

In the words of one of my heroes, Marcus Aurelius, *"If anyone can refute me — show me I'm making a mistake or looking at things from the wrong perspective — I'll gladly change. It's the truth I'm after, and the truth never harmed anyone. What harms us is to persist in self-deceit and ignorance."*

Ignorance is not bliss. Having a greater level of understanding, knowing how things work and why they are the way they are, is bliss.

2. "Finding" the time to read

How do people have time to go to the gym, work full time, go to school full time, while taking care of two kids? How are people able to quote every line off a reality T.V show, explain every event in the news (and the updates an hour later), and justify a recent divorce of a celebrity that doesn't even know you exist?

They create time to do those things.

Time has a deep correlation with priorities. If obtaining a flat stomach and six-pack abs is a major priority, you'll make time for it. If you're in bad health and your family is begging you through teary eyes to change your lifestyle, you'll make time to do so.

If you haven't read a book in years, reading ten in one year would be a major accomplishment — and a daunting one at that. So here's what I would recommend: *Dedicate an hour a day.* Start with that, and if necessary, do more. You can get a lot done in one, undistracted hour. Too much? 30 minutes a day, then next week try to a full sixty minutes.

Set a timer. This has helped me immensely. Turn off any distractions and read. It doesn't matter if you complete 5 pages or 50.

When I first started reading, it took me months to finish one book simply because my attention and desire to learn was so poor. But this got better over time through conscious effort. I went from reading roughly 50 pages a day, regardless of how long it took, to reading about 100-150 a day and not caring about the time it took. I loved doing it, so therefore it wasn't time wasted. It's part of my work.

Let's do some math:

- There are 365 days in a year, 24 hours in a day. That's a total of 8,760 hours in a year.

- If you dedicate one hour a day, that's 365 hours a year.

- That comes out to about 4% of all your hours used in a year.

- About 33% of all the time you use in a year is in sleep, assuming you get your 8 hours. *Only 4 percent for reading!* Now think about the stats on people watching television or the amount of time spent looking down at our phones.

- 4% becomes less daunting. It's a matter of perspective.

Mind you, this isn't a race or a badge of accomplishment. This is about the pursuit of understanding and exposure to different ideas and thoughts. This is about the kind of learning that stimulates your mind, exercises your creativity, and allows you to explore beyond your current boundaries. Through reading, you learn how to deal with adversity, failure, or tough choices. You see how others turned obstructions into opportunities — you relate with them. When you have this knowledge, this understanding, you should be motivated to use it in your own life.

3. Reading as a form of meditation

Reading a book is having a conversation. It's a deep meditation in your own mind — a discussion of thoughts, worldviews, and ideas. *It forces you to think.* When you think about a subject, say, the economy or culture, you're thinking only based on what you know, which is incredibly limited. When you read a book by someone who is more experienced than you are, someone who breathes and lives it, you're exposed to new patterns, ideas, stories, and perspectives — you're pushing the boundaries within your mind, lifting the fog of ignorance. Words, for as long as we've put them into existence, served one major function: *they move people.* Sitting, even for an hour a day, absorbing someone else's passionate words is moving, both physically and mentally.

Whenever I pick up a book, I prepare myself. I realize that the author has something important to say to me, something they *had* to share, and it may anger me or confuse me or amaze me. It isn't about being right, it's about asking questions and arriving at your own understanding. Why is the education system the way it is? Why did this company fail when this one was able to grow exponentially? Why does this design resonate whereas others don't? Why do people rationalize bad behavior? How can we catch ourselves in our own bubble?

Reading

Soon, it becomes exhilarating to read because you know that when you close the book you're going to be slightly different. You walk away knowing more than before. In essence, books are an endless supply for dots. It's the best way to learn a new subject because the author is writing from an understanding that took time to mold and develop. Once you have accumulated new dots and connected them, you're going to have new thoughts, a new perspective. It's likely that you will start reading books based on something you're currently going through — change in career, relationship, eating healthy, etc. You are now actively pursuing knowledge and wisdom. *You are learning, seeking new information—new dots—and connecting them.* The person you are when you open the book will always be different from the one who finishes it. **And that's because you have created a new picture by introducing and connecting new dots.**

4. With love and care

I'm a bit old school, so understand that this method doesn't have to be yours.

When I read, I have the book in front of me like an entree, a pen and highlighter and post-its as my utensils to help me devour the content. Yum.

When I read something that resonates with me, something that confuses or challenges or inspires me, I highlight it and write in the margins. I put a post-it on the top of the page that contains the markings and highlights, and I categorize it into keywords, i.e., Stoicism, Finance, Art, Business, Marketing, Psychology, or a huge question mark to remind me to go back to that section.

After I'm done with the book, I go back to the highlights and reread them. I transfer all my quotes and passage to a commonplace book (more on this later).

A great practice is to reread the same chapter, or read the same paragraph twice. Try it. You'll be surprised at what you missed, and you'll be glad that you returned to it.

In the words of Mortimer Adler, *"Marking a book is literally an expression of your differences or agreements with the author. It is the highest respect you can pay him."*

5. One book leads to five

Whenever I read a book, the author unfailingly mentions at least 5 other remarkable individuals. Education is also about **exploring**: traveling from one world to the next, and on the way forming your own opinion. If I'm reading a book on marketing, there may be research on neuroscience, or a book on psychology or anthropology.

READ THOSE BOOKS.

Write down the name of the author, look them up to see if they have a website where they provide resources or articles, and dive in. Read their books, and read the books that they recommend. This is a quintessential form of learning and it won't cost you nearly as much as college. It is challenging to do these things, hard to muster that motivation, hard to develop that habit or to see it as beneficial, but that's precisely the point: self-education builds discipline because many of us are so comfortable with having someone assign us work instead of actively exploring our own interests and discovering solutions to our problems.

6. The Fiction Fallacy

A lot of what I'm saying is seemingly focused on nonfiction, and to an extent it is; most of what I read is nonfiction. However, some of the greatest lessons that I've learned were through fiction. The kind of inspiration that a fiction story emits is enlightening.

The notion that *The Hunger Games* was about a rebel girl shooting arrows and taking down the government is shortsighted. The lessons about the needlessness of war, sacrifice, dealing with adversity, and the power in a community trying to change the status quo? That's more like it.

There's a hero in every story, and many times that hero could be you; or even better, there are characters in the story that are relatable to the people in your life. You can come to the conclusion, "I don't want to be like this person," or "I need to be more like this person." You're still learning even while being entertained, and that's precisely the point.

Throughout your studies, do not ignore fiction. Some of the most beautiful metaphors and lessons live in between the lines of a good story; the fact that you can discover it on your own shows the extent to which you're exercising your mind.

7. Read out of your comfort zone

Should you only study the subjects that interest you?

Connect The Dots

Here's my take on it: The reason you don't find something interesting is because you haven't connected this area of knowledge to your own life. Without that connection, there is no perceived benefit. How often did you say in school, "What is this class for? I'll never use it in my life." There are some subjects that immediately grasp your attention, whereas others you ponder the relevance and application.

Here's the catch: No subject is intrinsically boring. You may believe that math or Greek history or Chinese architecture isn't for you, but I'd say you're wrong. I think the greatest and most rewarding challenge is being able to take a seemingly lackluster subject and making it interesting by associating it to the things you deeply care about. The ability to connect seemingly unrelated dots, cross-pollinating bodies of knowledge, will ultimately make that boring subject into something relevant and profound.

The challenge is in the approach. By drawing connections to my interests and expertise, I am able to parse out the knowledge that is of use to me. Unearthing little gems of wisdom in subjects that you wouldn't think twice about is an educational joy. Besides, if you do this often, you'll have an archive of research that can be fruitful in your endeavors. Everyone already knows about Benjamin Franklin and Einstein and Henry Ford — find other remarkable people, their stories, the lessons, the dots, and connect them.

Ultimately, to make something fun, you have to ask the right questions.

Let's learn from a child.

In *Big Questions From Little People and Simple Answers From Brilliant Minds*, curated by Gemma Elwin Harris, she took thousands of

Reading

questions from children ages four to twelve. These questions were answered by some of the most brilliant minds of our time. Questions like, "Why is the sky blue?" or "Is it safe to eat worms?" or "Why are people mean?" My favorite of them all is one that epitomizes the lesson of this section. A brave, curious child asked, "Does Alexander The Great like frogs?"

What an interesting question! What made this child think of this? The answer comes from Bettany Hughes, a historian. She replies with great encouragement and enthusiasm (an attitude that we should embrace when teaching others). *"Your question has got me scratching my head and thinking all sorts of bizarre thoughts."* She thanks the kid for giving her a puzzle! When was the last time you felt gratitude for being asked a question? She answers:

Plato once said of the greeks, 'We live like frogs around a pond', because for the Greeks much of life — fighting, shopping, exchanging ideas — involved traveling across the Mediterranean sea. Aristophanes, a playwright from Athens, had a great success with his comedy called Frogs (written in 405 BC). And one of Aesop's fables, called 'The Boys and The Frogs', is about some mean boys throwing stones at frogs in a pond, meaning that what we do in fun often causes trouble for others.

Look at the dots that she gathered: Plato, Aristophanes, Aesop's fables, Greek history and how the Mediterranean sea facilitated fighting, communication, and trade.

So obviously these men in Ancient Greece actually spent a great deal of time thinking about frogs and talking about them. Why should Alexander be any different? Alexander loved Homer (he slept with a dagger and a copy of Homer's book the Iliad under his pillow). So there's the strong possibility he might also

Connect The Dots

have been aware of the comic epic Batrachomyomacia, 'The Battle of Frogs and Mice', which some people thought was by Homer.

The first thing to realize is that she kept an open mind. She's not slapping down any dots. Instead, she invites them because they have potential for connection. Because she dived into Ancient Greek history, she saw a pattern between thinkers, playwrights, stories, and history that mentions frogs.

And there's no doubt Alexander's experience of frogs would have extended beyond just reading about them. If you spend time in the Mediterranean away from the sounds of the twenty-first century (cars, trains, planes, mobile phones) and walk through the countryside, frogs make their presence felt in no uncertain terms, croaking and singing away in chorus. It can be like a frog opera out there.

The conclusion—the picture that is created—is hard to deny. There is such a rich assortment of dots that all amplify one another. The fact that these patterns are relatable reveals some validity to this question. Unless there is a direct quote from Alexander the Great professing his love for frogs, we may truly never know for sure. But, by using the dots that are available, we can begin connecting them to create a picture that has potential for answering very unique and challenging questions.

Thank you for your question — I'll never think of Alexander in quite the same way again.

Curiosity is the panacea to boredom. If you are having a hard time connecting a dull body of knowledge to your endeavors, keep asking yourself questions and don't sleep until you find at least a glimmer of an answer.

Reading

Understanding > Being Right

I'll be the first to admit it: I'm not very smart. There's so much that I have to learn, so many dots that I have yet to connect, so much more that I need to understand.

When I first started writing this book in the beginning of 2013, what was intended to be strategies and meditations on self-education actually ended up as an ignorant rant about the system at large. I wrote nearly 20,000 words and the feedback was exactly what I didn't want it to be. I put the project on hold and took a few months off. I dedicated many months to study the education system in its entirety. My first moment of self-awareness was this: I don't know enough about this system. I was failing to connect the dots and led to frustration and misplaced expectations. My mental model wasn't complete. If someone were to ask me, "why do you think school is the way it is?" I wouldn't have had an educated, thoughtful response. What did I know? What had I tried to learn? What dots did I obtain and connect? The answer was embarrassing.

I looked into the history of the educational system, the Industrial Era, and looked up experts in the education/political field that expressed concerns, doubts, and solutions to mass education. Remember how I said how one book leads to many more? I read *Out of Our Minds* by Sir Ken Robinson, a pioneer in education, and that lead to more books, research, and people focused on changing that ecosystem. By connecting all of these dots, my frustration for mass education was alleviated as my understanding deepened. My expectations and beliefs changed. My thinking changed. A new picture formed, one that I previously couldn't have imagined. I was now ready to write a book that helped people, that provided a solution instead of yelling about a system.

Connect The Dots

The same goes for other topics of study: The more I learn about psychology, the more I learn about people, business, and how irrational I really am. The more I learn about philosophy, the more I realize how difficult it is to act on principles instead of moods. The more I learn about design and marketing, the more I learn about human nature and communication. The more I learn about the brain, in the words of Marcus Aurelius, the more I am attentive of the power inside me and worship it sincerely.

Many of us lack understanding and **we are afraid to admit it**. It's far easier to complain about the life we aren't living instead of realizing that our shortcomings stem from a lack of understanding. That's the ultimate problem that we face.

And how do we fix a lack of understanding? Through education. Through studying what we're interested in or what we're repelled by. Through looking at the world with different perspectives. Whenever I get emails from readers or questions from friends about what they could be doing to improve their lives, I tell them to start reading books. Reading is a gateway to other people's worldview. It's about putting on someone else's glasses and seeing the world through their eyes.

I'm not saying that only reading books will transform you into this great human being. One book won't make you smarter any more than a single salad will make you skinnier. Developing the habit of reading is a profound shift not only in your daily routine but in your mind. Think about it: What do you consume all day? The news, Facebook statuses from people you don't talk to anymore, email? How will your thinking shift when you set aside even one hour of that focus to read something that can actually enrich your life?

Reading

Start diving into books and disciplining yourself to think beyond your comfort zone. Every time I finish a book I walk away knowing more than before — a different understanding, new ideas, and the ability to connect patterns that I noticed in other areas of my life and studies. It compels me to make better choices, to be more empathic, and helps me connect with others.

Last piece of advice: Always carry a book with you. Don't read Instagram, read a book. A book is a documentation of a personal experience. Instagram or whatever social media you use may be fun, even useful, but ask yourself, *What are you learning that is helping you evolve?*

"Laws, wisely administered, will secure men in the enjoyment of the fruits of their labour, whether of mind or body, at a comparatively small personal sacrifice; but no laws, however stringent, can make the idle industrious, the thriftless provident, or the drunken sober. Such reforms can only be effected by means of individual action, economy, and self-denial; by better habits, rather than by greater rights."

— Samuel Smiles

"Put your pens down and listen!"

As important as reading is, it is not the only avenue by which you can further your self-education. And, like reading, it is something you probably don't do enough of.

Listening is one of the greatest skills you can have in your business and personal life. Yet for so many of us it is woefully underdeveloped. For nearly our entire educational experience, "listening" actually meant "copying"; furiously writing lectures verbatim for the fear of missing out on information that could make or break our grades. Yes, our hands would feel like they were about to fall off at the end of class but we assumed that our notes were the key to a coveted letter grade. Forget learning. Forget internalizing information and reaching our own understanding. We wanted the answer to the test questions! Of course we forgot the material at the end of the semester, why wouldn't we? We weren't listening during class, we were only copying.

I love listening to interviews and podcasts. It is such a great way to expose yourself to a world of people doing different things. Srinivas Rao, the host of The Unmistakable Creative, interviews authors, entrepreneurs, bloggers, creatives, and more. These 45 to 60 minute interviews provide a plethora of wisdom, strategies, and information. You

"Put your pens down and listen!"

can listen to how someone built themself up, how they recovered from failure or why they specifically failed, and what they're working on or recently released. You can find patterns and connect the dots.

No matter what kind of podcasts or interviews you listen to, each individual has a unique perspective on the topic they're talking about. You don't have to agree with what they say, but nevertheless it helps you differentiate the information and how it pertains to you. You may not agree with what is being said but that perspective is a new dot and so is your reaction to it. It's not about being right, it's about understanding what resonates with you, your personality, desires, aspirations, and life. Whether you love or hate what is being said, dots are still being connected. Be open to new opinions. Be flexible. The pursuit of understanding is about being fluid, open-minded and, if necessary, adapting.

Throughout these interviews you'll find someone that you can relate to, someone that struggled the way you are and is succeeding in the way you want to be. Learn from them. Contact them. Ask questions of your own. Visit their website, subscribe to them if they provide value, and study all of it. Inadvertently, you'll discover more people through this one person — and so continues the momentum of educational exploration. More than half of my mentors are people I've never met in person. We keep in contact through email and their guidance is every bit as impactful as it would be if we met face to face.

Note: I don't take notes when I'm listening. The entire point of this exercise is for you to *listen*, to churn the thoughts in mind, and to think deeply. The point is to be attentive to the discussion, not frantically trying to copy it down. If an interview overwhelms me, I'll listen to it again and write down a few key takeaways.

Connect The Dots

It's sad that many of us have allowed such a valuable skill to languish. But of course it's not too late to exercise our ability to listen. I have listed my favorite podcasts in the Resources section of this book. I hope you use my suggestions but also find some valuable ones on your own. All of these are valuable dots that will help you deliver your own great presentation.

Keep in mind:

- Listen to what the host has to say. Does he or she mention people, research, or ideas? How does the host deliver information? What patterns can you find that are responsible for the guest's success? How, exactly, did they earn 100,000 or 1 million listeners? There is so much to be learned outside of the interview itself.

- Interviewers/podcasters often ask great questions that elicit even greater responses. Asking questions is vital to your education. Learn how to ask really great questions by listening to the people who do it for a living.

- Take notes, sure, but don't turn this into a transcription exercise. If you're training to be a court stenographer, go for it. If not, treat this is an exercise in listening and thinking. You can always rewind.

- Almost every podcaster I know has a website or a social media profile. If you find great value in their content, explore further. Visit their site, see who they're following or subscribed to, and find another teacher.

- Finding podcasts is simple. I go on iTunes, go into the store, click on podcasts, and search. Keywords like "interview", "business",

"Put your pens down and listen!"

"marketing", and "career" will bring up many results. From there you can pick what interests you, listen, and if you like it, subscribe. Better still, most podcasts are free.

- Once you find one amazing podcast, you're likely to be exposed to others, or at the very least some interesting people. Leverage that and expand your archive of educational material.

"You are the steward of your own potential. The resources within you — and around you — are only tapped when you recognize their value and develop ways to use them. Whatever the future of technology may hold, the greatest leaders will be those most capable of tuning into themselves and harnessing the full power of their own minds." — Scott Belsky

Building An Engine of Knowledge

As crazy as it may sound, blogs saved my life.

When I was building my blog, all of my research and resources came from the Internet. There were no textbooks or classes that I could take at my university. I even tried majoring in journalism. It ended quickly.

One day, while desperately searching through Google, I landed on Copyblogger — a blog that provides rich content about online marketing, blogging, and tips on nearly every tactic and tool that a blog or online business may use. But that's just a small portion of what they do. They sell software, WordPress themes, and online courses. You buy the product and they provide the education for free. They're not only selling you something, they're teaching you every conceivable thing about it. Genius. This single site provided me with more relevant marketing education than the entire course catalog at my university. And this is just one blog. There are thousands out there accomplishing the same thing in different ways:

Blogs helped me to build my business and establish my online brand. They have also taught me to lead a healthier life. In the midst of a self-improvement phase, I was immediately captivated by a very popular blog called ZenHabits. Leo's journey of losing weight, changing his habits, getting out of debt, quitting cigarettes, becoming vegetarian, and living more mindfully were an inspiration. It was such an amazing opportunity to learn. His blog gave me the desire and the strategies to implement positive change in my own life.

When I go looking for new blogs, I ask myself a few questions to help me differentiate what was right for me and what wasn't. Yours may vary, but here's a start:

- Who is the author(s) and what is their story? In my opinion, the more vulnerable the writing is, the better the blog is.

- What kind of value are they sharing?

- What problems are they helping me solve?

- What has this person accomplished?

- Are they consistent?

- Are they exposing me to different people and ideas?

Subscribe to blogs that are relevant to your endeavors and build out from there.

I have provided a long list of the websites and blogs that I use and find interesting and helpful in the Resources section of this book. The rest is up to you.

Connect The Dots

Organize Your Engine of Knowledge

Now, what do we do with all of these sites and valuable content?

We organize it.

Feedly is a tool that helps you build the engine of knowledge that I'm talking about. Instead of having multiple browsers opened up, I use Feedly to organize all the websites that I'm subscribed to.

But Feedly isn't the only option. There are alternatives, many of which you can find by in this article.

Here's a few things to consider:

- Sign Up for the Newsletter: Whenever you find a blog that is useful, subscribe to it through your RSS reader. Also, look for the site's newsletter and sign up. Many of the blogs that I'm subscribed offer extremely valuable content in the newsletter that isn't available on the site. I've gotten amazing deals on books, services and opportunities (like internships, freelance work, etc.) through these emails.

- Research Guest Contributors: Does this blog have guest contributors? If so, visit their sites as well. The idea is to have a diverse ecosystem that fulfills your needs. If you find yourself reading only one subject, then this is an easy way to expand and cross-pollinate ideas.

- Read and Share the Content: Remember that reading blogs takes up time. Subscribing to 100 blogs won't make you smarter if you don't use the information. Be attentive to each post that you read. Let it percolate in your mind. And don't believe everything you read — challenge it, question it, form your own opinion, and if you still like what you read, then be sure to share it with someone who can benefit from it.

- Follow Industry Leaders: Finding great blogs naturally leads to great books, ideas, and people. It will expose you to a multitude of stories and expertise. By following the smart industry leaders, thinkers and doers, you can learn from them, or even better, get in touch with them.

- Make the Time: I usually catch up with all my blogs either in the morning or later at night. Most of my hardcore focused reading is during the day. I'm not saying to follow my methodology, but once you build this engine of knowledge, you have to make it a priority to keep it up. Learning should be a part of your daily routine, even if that means scheduling the time for it.

- Make It Manageable: You can only know yourself by testing yourself. At first, I was subscribed to about 50 blogs. This became too overwhelming and I ended up not reading most of them. By cutting the fat, I could focus only on the valuable stuff, the subjects that I truly want to learn deeply about. So if you think you can keep up with 50 blogs, then go for it. But if you find yourself not reading any, then it may be to a cue to tone it down a bit.

Your engine of knowledge will serve as one of your greatest tools. My blog feed exposes me to information on marketing, design, creativity, psychology, culture, anthropology, writing, art, philosophy — and just recently, architecture, drawing, and neuroscience. All of these subjects are likely to change as my interests evolve. There's so much useful

Connect The Dots

information out there, and day after day it's expanding. Organizing your engine of knowledge and prioritizing your time to use it will keep that valuable content within reach.

In a way, the organization of your engine of knowledge serves as a mental model for how you're connecting of dots. Take a step back and look at what you read regularly. Are you expanding your horizons? Are you playing around with new, unchallenged subjects? Leverage this tool wisely. It will expose you to great thinkers, doers, ideas, stories, and information. Every dot has a potential for connection.

"The active pursuit of truth is our proper business. We have no excuse for conducting it badly or unfittingly. But failure to capture our prey is another matter. For we are born to quest after it; to possess it belongs to a greater power. Truth is not, as Democritus said, hidden in the depths of the abyss, but situated rather at an infinite height in the divine understanding. The world is but a school of inquiry." — Michel De Montaigne

Consciously Curating Your Channels

The other day I unfollowed almost everyone on Twitter.

It was harder than I expected. I felt weird, especially when unfollowing people that I knew. What would they think? Would they take it personally?

Many months have gone by and no one has said anything to me. I still have my friends. So that's the answer: No, they might not take it personally, and if they do then you need new friends.

I have no idea why I was following half the people that I did — wait, yes I do: I followed them because they followed me first. But after years of doing this, my stream of information has been voyeuristic at best and soul-sucking at worst. I caught myself becoming bitter because of the kinds of the tweeted information I was consuming daily. The medium was influencing my thoughts, and in turn, my life.

There is a reason for this obsessive compulsive finger-dancing on guerrilla glass. Tiffany Shlain, one of the many contributors for the book *Manage Your Day-to-Day*, explains it on an evolutionary level: *"All of these forms of communication are extensions of us. Going back to [the visionary philosopher of communication theory] Marshall McLuhan: everything is an extension of our desire for connection. We couldn't see far enough, we invented the telescope. We wanted to communicate across distances, we invented the telephone. Then, we wanted to connect with everyone and share all these ideas, and we invented the Internet. We've created this global brain that is very much an extension of our own brains. And because it's an extension of us, it's good and it's bad—because we're both good and bad. We're both focused and distracted. So I think the real problem isn't the technology. I think we need to evolve to know when to turn it off."*

Even better, we ought to be responsible for the stream of information bombarding our daily lives by consciously curating our channels to facilitate education, wisdom, and ideas. I'm going to show you how.

This all comes down to preference: What do you enjoy using?

I don't like Facebook for a variety of reasons. And I'm pretty awful at LinkedIn. Twitter is my preference because of the way it's designed. I can follow people or businesses or movements. I can unfollow at any time. I have private lists that allow me to get all the relevant information that *I want to see*. It works for me.

I'm going to share my social media principles. Of course, yours may vary and I hope they do. Having a personal philosophy for something as addicting and personal as social media helps you draw a line:

- Subscribe to Valuable Content: Just like reading a good book or finding an interesting blog, one smart person leads to many more. So whatever you're using — Twitter, LinkedIn, Facebook, Tumblr, Instagram — the idea is to follow people who provide and share great value. *How are they helping you solve a problem or become well versed on subject?* Many of the smart people I follow on Twitter aren't focused on promoting their work, but the work of others. They're sharing what they're learning, reading, discovering, etc.

- Explore the Accounts of Those You Admire: I love Twitter because I can see who other people are following. This is a fantastic way to build your database of wisdom: who are your heroes/mentors/aspirations learning from? Follow them, too.

- Assign Different Tools to Different Purposes: Some tools serve greater functions than others. So if I want to become inspired through pictures, I'll use Instagram or Tumblr. I'll only follow the profiles that provide inspiration and allow me to steal ideas. Twitter may not be the best tool for this, but that's just my opinion. The idea is to make the tool work for you — and you do this by curating it based on your own interests and understanding how it fits in your educational strategy.

- Designate Social Media Outlets for Different Things: I have plenty of friends on social media, but I don't follow them on Twitter if they don't play a role in my education by sharing articles, books, or interesting people that they're learning from. If I want to know what they're eating, I'll ask or join them. Instagram is where I follow friends, food recipes, yogis, and fitness lovers — and that's all. My Twitter is focused on following journalists, entrepreneurs, writers, scientists, psychologists, educators, and more. If I had relatives in Korea, I'd probably use Facebook, but alas, I don't.

Being conscious of what we view on our screens — something we look at for most of our day — is an important challenge that must be acknowledged and administered. It's easy to get lost in the heap of distractions, irrelevant bits of information, ranting, trolling, and more.

James Victor, a brilliant contributor to the book, *Manage Your Day-to-Day*, says it much better than I do: *"Our fun and well-designed portables have got their hooks so deep in us that they are changing our manners and our culture. We no longer see phone calls, IMs, or a "ping" as an intrusion into our personal time and space. The gym and the park are no longer places for personal development or reflection, but just another place to "check in." It used to be that taking a phone call while at the dinner table or on the john was seen as incredibly bad manners or a sign of mental illness. Now it's commonplace and acceptable. Self-respect and etiquette are being nudged out of our lives in lieu of convenient connection. Even work has no time or place and spills out all over our personal lives.*

[...]

The crux of this problem is that we are losing the distinction between urgent and important — now everything gets heaped in the urgent pile. And it's quite frankly easier to do the trivial things that are "urgent" than it is to do the important things. But when we choose urgent over important, what we're really choosing is other people's priorities over our own. With every new e-mail, we become like the leaves in the wind, reacting to any breeze willy-nilly. We quickly set aside our own concerns to attend to those of others. This busywork pulls out attention from the meaningful work — taking time to think, reflect, and imagine. Yet, it's these pauses that make our lives better and lay the groundwork for our greatest accomplishments."

Creativity, education, art, and innovation are some of the most powerful forces that are changing our world: one app, one website, one service, and one story at a time. Stuffing your face with information that serves no greater purpose other than to entertain your fears or let you peak into someone else's miserable day stifles creativity and self-sovereignty. We reserve no time for creating, learning, thinking, and reflecting, but instead, only consuming, criticizing, and comparing.

The challenge isn't to find better tools to lead a more productive life, it's learning to be mindful of the tools that have already taken root. Mindfulness while using technology is important, and therefore the future belongs to those who can tame their distractions.

"To be shaken out of the ruts of ordinary perception, to be shown for a few timeless hours the outer and the inner world, not as they appear to an animal obsessed with work and notions, but as they are apprehended, directly and unconditionally, by Mind at Large—this is an experience of inestimable value to everyone." — Aldous Huxley

The Commonplace Book

We've established an effective way to organize the information you find online but what do you do with all of the information you learn away from the computer?

Memorizing all of it is impossible, of course, so the next best thing is a commonplace book that allows you to collect, store, and refer back to the wisdom and information found throughout your studies.

In the words of Ryan Holiday [you can find the article here. I highly recommend it]: *"A commonplace book is a central resource or depository for ideas, quotes, anecdotes, observations and information you come across during your life and didactic pursuits. The purpose of the book is to record and organization these gems for later use in your life, in your business, in your writing, speaking or whatever it is that you do.*

Some of the greatest men and women in history have kept these books. Marcus Aurelius kept one — which more or less became the Meditations. Petrarch kept one. Montaigne, who invented the essay, kept a handwritten compilation of sayings, maxims and quotations from literature and history that he felt were important. His earliest essays were little more than compilations of these thoughts. Thomas Jefferson kept one. Napoleon kept one. HL Mencken, who did so much for the English language, as his biographer put it, "methodically filled notebooks with incidents, recording straps of dialog and slang" and favorite bits from newspaper columns he liked. Bill Gates keeps one."

Right now, I can slide my finger across my iPhone, tap on Evernote, and have a database of my learning — from quotes or metaphors on managing adversity, marketing principles to abide to, habits of famous writers, inventions that transformed cultures — I have instant access to it all. If I need to use a powerful quote, story, or metaphor for my writing or projects, I can share multiple points of view from a range of expertise, people, and history. It's simply amazing. My commonplace book was responsible for many of the quotes and ideas for this book, making the process less daunting and allowing me to cross-pollinate ideas. When it came to writing papers for school, I already had a plethora of studies — citations and all — available at my disposal. It made the process effortless.

How to Organize and Fill Your Commonplace Book

A commonplace book enhances your self-education journey, and should be put into practice *immediately*. I've listed my own strategy below.

The idea is to get in the practice of adding something to your commonplace book everyday. After years of doing this, you'll have a vault of wisdom — perhaps one of the most priceless items that you'll ever own. Your commonplace book will supplement all your creative, personal and professional endeavors.

Here are some of my principles for building a commonplace book:

- I highlight, write in the margins, and leave post-its on the top of the page. Each post-it (or margin note) contains short phrases or keywords to remind me of what that specific passage or quote was about. Sometimes I'll write questions that I want to revisit, or I'll remind myself to connect this idea with another from a book that I read.

- Once I finish a book, I don't look at it for about a week. When I return to it, I transfer all my notes into Evernote. This is also a way to reread a book so that the information is repeated in your mind. After all, rehearsal is good for memory. You're most likely highlighting what you think is important, so rereading the parts that resonated with you will help you learn and remember them better — and possibly discover a tidbit of wisdom that you missed the first time around.

- When I find an online article that is incredibly insightful, I'll write the headline, add the link, and extract specific quotes or passages that were helpful and add them underneath.

- Mind you, **you don't have to use Evernote**. Ryan Holiday uses index cards and organizes them into boxes. Maria Popova uses Tumblr and calls it Explore (but also made Evernote an integral part of her work). Others may use Moleskins or plain notebooks. Find what works for you. I use both Evernote and a Moleskin.

- I organize all my notes into main keywords and meticulously tag them: Finance, Art, How Writer's Write, Marketing, Education, Self-awareness, Inventions, etc. It makes it easier to search and find what you're looking for. Throughout your life you can always go back to these notes and use them however you wish. Instead of Googling something, you'll have more concrete stories and information, and the source you obtained it from.

The Commonplace Book

- I don't write only the quote or passage, but also add a sentence or two before it explaining how this passage was introduced, or better, how I would introduce it to someone. This is great for tagging keywords and makes everything easier to find.

- I always add the author's name, title of the book or article or study, and page number after the passage. Throughout my studies, whenever I want to properly reference it, I can go to the source and find what I'm looking for.

- When I read Kindle books, I treat ebook passages the same way. Yes, Kindle provides a copy-and-paste shortcut, but I still take the time to write the sentences into my commonplace book. It is something I take a lot of joy in. This is a way of **writing to learn**. You're feeling through your fingers how a person created this thought, this sentence, this passage, and why it ultimately moved you. I think it's a great practice. You owe it to your education to not take the shortcut.

- Whenever you're having trouble with something, go back to your commonplace book. I can't tell you how many times I struggled with something in my life like failure or uncertainty, only to open up my Evernote, go to the notes filed under Adversity or Dealing With Reality, and be reminded of principles that guide me to fruitful outcomes. It's like having all of your teachers' wisdom close at hand.

The key to properly utilizing a tool like the commonplace book is to ingrain it into your daily habits, almost like a ritual. Every time you read something interesting on the web or find a remarkable passage in a book or hear a sentence that seduces your mind, your next course of action should be to record it. The commonplace book is a timeless,

Connect The Dots

fruitful archive of all the wisdom and information you come across in your studies; everything you felt was worth remembering, sharing, or using in the future. It is a guide to your way of thinking and living, a record of your growth, a source of reminders, and a tool that will enhance both your work and life.

"But the upside of painful knowledge is so much greater than the downside of blissful ignorance."

— Sheryl Sandberg

Don't Just Absorb But Also Apply

"Writing is thinking," said two-time Pulitzer Prize winner David McCullough. "To write well is to think clearly. That's why it's hard."

It's easy to believe that reading 100 books and listening to great interviews will make you smarter. To an extent it will. The idea of absorbing knowledge and wisdom is so that you can apply it to your life. Application of knowledge gained from your didactic pursuit will ultimately transform you.

I write to learn. My blog, which was once an audience of one, grew into a community that was interested in learning about the topics that I enjoy writing about. The topics revolve around mastery, technology, self-awareness, mindfulness, dealing with adversity, psychology and philosophy — and because I naturally expanded to other areas of knowledge — I cross-pollinate these ideas to write about the problems or issues that confuse or elude me. If I have trouble understanding habits, I'll read a book about it, I'll have previous notes on, say, writer's habits or athlete's habits, and I'll write an article on it. Not only am I educating myself and seeing how I'm thinking, but I'm also providing value for others — sharing a perspective and relevant knowledge; helping you connect the dots.

Don't Just Absorb But Also Apply

To reinforce the connections in our mind, we must think, apply, experiment, and discuss the information. How you do this depends on your preference for learning. When I am learning something new, I essentially collect a diverse range of dots from all the different books and interviews I have read. Now I have all this information sitting in my head. I have started to make connections and it kind of makes sense. I can understand these new ideas, but if I were to present it or try to teach someone, it wouldn't be effective. I haven't articulated my stance on it yet, I haven't fully realized my picture based on the different notions and facts. By writing about it, interjecting my own personal experiences, deeply thinking about the information and how it connects, I strengthen the connection between the dots. Through writing, I may have an insightful breakthrough that clarifies the idea for me and deepens my understanding.

If writing is thinking, which I agree it is, then through writing you can understand your level of comprehension; you know where you stand. This was a moment of self-awareness for me: When I was writing articles on mastery and why it was must be pursued to lead a meaningful life, I realized that my understanding was incredibly amateur. It was frustrating. As I was rereading my draft I thought to myself, "Wow, really, is this how I'm thinking about this subject?" Through writing and reading, you can refine your thinking. When it comes time to present something to your colleagues or boss, you're showing that your level of understanding is evolving and that you're putting effort into it. Even better, if you can connect seemingly unrelated dots and tell an interesting story, you're now entering the realm of new discoveries and igniting minds.

A few ways you can write to learn is to have a blog. You don't have to make it public. This is for your own educational journey. You can do this on your Evernote, and write in a way that is teaching someone. You can create a Tumblr. You can go Blogger.com. You can use Medium.com to share your thoughts — hey, someone might really like what you're thinking about. The idea is to focus on a topic and write about it. How are you thinking? And what can you do to improve it? In what areas does it seem that you lack an understanding? What areas are you strong in?

Absorbing all kinds of worldviews and wisdom lays down a great foundation, but what is a foundation without building something on top of it?

"We can pick our teachers and we can pick our friends and we can pick the books we read and the music we listen to and the movies we see, etcetera. You are a mashup of what you let into your life."

— Paula Scher

Connect Your Dots

Connecting your dots is about how you think, learn, and apply your knowledge and experience to ideas. It is an ability that is unique to the way you obtain and organize information, see the world, and apply what you know. Think about it in terms of books: There are countless books on the topics of marketing, health, and business. Why so many? Because each author has connected a wide range of dots that ultimately creates their perspective on that topic. They use their own personal experiences, research, and the patterns that they've noticed throughout their lives. In short, a piece of work — a business, software, app, book, or online service — represents someone's mental model. Each book, or interview you listen to, or class that you take, or a video that you watch may provide a missing piece to the picture. The way you connect the dots will always be different than the person next to you, and that's an opportunity because this leaves room for intelligent discussions and for potential dots to be uncovered and connected by their differing perspective.

Self-education is not a fad, the same way connecting the dots is not a talent. This isn't a one month diet; this is about embracing a new lifestyle. The more you relentlessly connect the dots, the further you go on your path of self-education.

Like anything worthwhile, self-education requires deliberate practice and the right mindset. The proper mindset is vital because it's not directly taught in traditional education. Rarely do teachers or professors say, "Hey, the Internet is the richest resource available to you right now; here's how to use it." It is seemingly self-evident that we will master these tools and resources because we grow up alongside of them, and that's where I disagree.

The three basic elements that build the mindset for self-education are:

- Take initiative

- Desire to learn

- Be Teachable

Initiative

Charles Darwin developed the theory of evolution not by sitting in a classroom, but through a voyage that he embarked on after countless failed attempts at finding his purpose. *"Nothing could have been worse for the development of my mind,"* he said, *"the school as a means of education for me was a complete blank."* Indeed, his father pushed him to pursue medicine or to be a member of the clergy — all of which Darwin disdained. He recalled his father saying, *"You care for nothing but shooting, dogs, and rat-catching, and you will be a disgrace to yourself and all your family."* A former professor told him about a ship that was about to leave port, the HMS *Beagle*. They needed a biologist to collect specimen to send back to England. Darwin volunteered, and in South America he collected a multitude of specimens, which in turn, motivated him to think about the origin of species. After five years at sea — a voyage that would transform him inside and out — he devoted his life to developing the theory of evolution, one of the single greatest ideas ever presented to humanity.

Connect The Dots

The first element here is initiative. No one forced him to go on a five-year voyage. Darwin saw an opportunity and took it, the same way you can take this opportunity to begin the path of self-education. Throughout his experience, he was slowly connecting the dots. Every destination motivated him to examine the ecosystem, and to think about his theory and the origin of life. Over the span of five years, so many dots were collected, and in turn, connected. A picture was forming. He was able to describe it in detail. It made sense to him and therefore he endeavored to have it make sense to the public.

The only challenge that you're facing right now is starting, building the habit, adding it to your To-Do list. From the moment you close this book, you have collected many dots on the topic of self-education. Some dots will resonate, some won't. There are, of course, other books on this topic. There is nothing stopping you from starting a commonplace book, purchasing books to further your education, and spending 30 minutes to write about what you learned — *that* is initiative. Once you commit, a habit begins to form. Once a habit is formed, your life will start to change.

Desire to Learn

I'm sure you can think of at least five people who dropped out of school and blazed their own trails — people who took their education into their own hands, and more importantly, *learned by doing*. After all, we love praising these heroes for going against the tide. This isn't something you're born with, it's something that you build yourself to become. Some argue that they're geniuses or that they have something that we don't but I don't buy into that.

I believe that **the desire to learn** is the lifeblood of learning, and, ultimately, the key to living a great life. We inadvertently connect the dots throughout our lives simply because that's how our brains work. But through a deliberate and disciplined practice, we can take control of the process and avoid the comfortable mistake of waiting for things to happen.

In the words of Robert Greene [emphasis by me]: *"The basic elements of this story are repeated in the lives of all of the great Masters in history: a youthful passion or predilection, a chance encounter that allows them to discover how to apply it, an apprenticeship in which they come alive with energy and focus. They excel by their ability to practice harder and move faster through the process, all of this stemming **from the intensity of their desire to learn** and from the deep connection they feel to their field of study. And at the core of this intensity of effort is a quality that is genetic and inborn—not talent or brilliance, which must be developed, but rather a deep and powerful inclination toward a particular subject."*

What makes you come alive with energy and focus? What topic or area makes your mind buzz? This intense desire to learn and explore will ultimately be responsible for the development of yourself and your craft — it will aid in breaking past plateaus and reaching a kind of understanding unmatched to most. The challenge of our times is discovering or rediscovering that powerful inclination and realizing that the intense desire to learn plus the pursuit of mastery paves the road to a meaningful life.

In my observations, the smartest and successful people have this desire. It is ruthlessly unquenchable. Even after attaining the kind of success that could make us seethe with envy, they continue to learn, refine, and adapt. There isn't an arrogant confidence that they know everything there is to know, but rather an honest level of humility that continuously fuels this desire to learn. This is what makes them great.

If we were to fuse the elements of initiative and a desire to learn into two words: Be teachable.

Be Teachable

Think about my own experience: I wanted to write about my opinions about the video games that I was playing. I was already capable of stringing words together in coherent sentences and I had a solid understanding of my subject matter. The opportunity to learn blogging from the pros was all over the Internet. Listening to interviews and podcasts, voraciously devouring books, absorbing the content on blogs, asking questions through the comment section or emails, getting published on sites with large audiences, even failing on a handful of projects — these were all little apprenticeships that developed my mind and honed my skills. The true key to my development, however, was the **willingness to change my mind**.

Perhaps this is one of the most important and arduous elements in the journey of self-education: allowing yourself to think differently and **a readiness to change what you believe**.

While Maria Popova was a college student working four jobs to pay for school, she compiled stimulating reads on a variety of topics to share with her coworkers. This experiment, which she called Brain Pickings in her email subject line, is now featured in the Library of Congress digital archive of "materials of historical importance." She is a writer whose ethic, desire, and habits make me question if I am working to my full potential. I read her blog everyday, sometimes the same post twice.

She admonishes: *"Allow yourself the uncomfortable luxury of changing your mind. Cultivate that capacity for "negative capability." We live in a culture where one of the greatest social disgraces is not having an opinion, so we often form our 'opinions' based on superficial impressions or the borrowed ideas of others, without investing the time and thought that cultivating true conviction necessitates. We then go around asserting these donned opinions and clinging to them as anchors to our own reality. It's enormously disorienting to simply say, 'I don't know.' But it's infinitely more rewarding to understand than to be right — even if that means changing your mind about a topic, an ideology, or, above all, yourself."*

To be **teachable** is to be open to new and foreign ideas. To allow dots to enter into the mind and simmer. It's about letting curiosity take the lead, introducing you to new thoughts, beliefs, and patterns. *It is about evolving your understanding.* It's not about surrendering or blindly accepting, it's about playing with the ideas, opinions, beliefs, and worldviews that you encounter. This kind of humility facilitates learning. It's wise to start viewing your education integral to your life. It must become the lifeblood of all that you do, like breathing and drinking water. Without it, you wither, grow cold, and fail to adapt to your ceaselessly changing environment.

Initiative, a desire to learn, and to be teachable — these are principles that guide self-education. It's what has guided me for all these years. It was responsible for reinventing my life. It is what will keep your mind fluid and malleable, not closed and concrete. The relentless practice of connecting the dots will ultimately help you form mental models, and later on, to improve them with richer detail. The greater the detail, the greater your understanding. And a greater understanding alleviates frustrations, false expectations, and self-defeating delusions.

Whether you're in school or not, whether you're about to enroll into a new semester or about to drop out of one, I hope I sparked a visceral desire to pursue education as if your life depended on it. Traditional education may not be for everyone, but learning is indeed a part of what it means to be human. It champions growth, evolution, and change. Like Maria Popova said, it's not about being right, it's about understanding. Too often we expend so much energy on hate and frustration, when all this time the panacea to our imprisonment of ignorance is relieved in the pursuit of understanding. I've learned to fall in love with that word — *understanding* — because an understanding shows that we are connecting the dots in our mind, even if we disagree with the idea. We are considering the different perspectives, ideas, factors, and more. An understanding is what we must actively pursue and develop in a disciplined way to lead a great life. An understanding is how civilizations moved forward, how science reached breakthroughs, and how humans achieved the impossible. I hope that you reconnect with your inclination, I hope that you pursue learning everyday as if it was a part of your diet, I hope that you are open to changing mind and yourself, and most of all, I hope that you make a difference.

"Walk tall, kick ass, learn to speak Arabic, love music and never forget you come from a long line of truth seekers, lovers and warriors."

— Hunter S. Thompson

Resources

Below will contain a long list of all the websites and blogs that I use or have used in my self-educational pursuits. Remember: one person or website can lead you to a few more. Let curiosity be at the forefront. Explore. Challenge. Connect dots. Ask questions. Never settle or get too comfortable. In the words of Bruce Lee, *"Be like water, my friend."*

Videos

Seth Godin on STOP STEALING DREAMS. What Is School For?

Sir Ken Robinson on Changing Education Paradigms.

The Future of Learning by Ericsson.

Build a School In The Cloud by Sugatra Mitra, winner of the TED 2013 Prize.

Online Courses

Coursera (https://www.coursera.org): This is what they call a MOOC (Massive Open Online Course). Coursera has over 5 million students and 500 classes. They partnered with top universities and organizations to offer free online courses ranging in a multitude of subjects.

Resources

The co-founder did a fascinating TEDTalk(http://www.ted.com/talks/daphne_koller_what_we_re_learning_from_online_education.html) on the growth of Coursera and the rise of online education. I've used Coursera to supplement my time at school and to take courses that were interesting. Did I finish all of them? No, because my goal wasn't mastery but rather to entertain my childish curiosity.

CreativeLive (http://www.creativelive.com/about): Imagine being able to learn from an expert in your field? CreativeLive offers real-time online workshops with experts from many industries — photography, business, marketing, design, writing, and more. You can watch for free by participating in the live course or you can purchase it later.

edX (https://www.edx.org): You can take a class on the Principles of Written English from UC Berkley, Innovation in Healthcare from Harvard, and learn about Wiretaps and Big Data from a professor at Cornell. All for free. Founded by Harvard and MIT, edX is a non-profit online organization that provides access to top tier university courses.

Skillshare (http://www.skillshare.com): I started getting back into pencil drawing and had a hard time finding a local workshop. Through Skillshare, I was able to find an incredible online drawing course for $20. With 17 video lessons and the ability to ask the teacher questions, I most likely saved myself hundreds of dollars. This site has everything from drawing to starting a business.

Lynda (http://www.lynda.com): If you want to learn coding, design, photoshop, programming, 3D animation and more, this is the site to go to.

Khan Academy (http://www.khanacademy.org): This is a very popular and big MOOC and one of the first ones I started using. The principles are similar to that of the previously mentioned sites, but also offers classes as early as third grade math, like addition and subtraction. From stats, achievements, an online community, video tutorials, and classroom data, this is another platform that facilities self-education and will continuously grow with time.

Websites/Blogs/Podcasts

I honestly wish I could name all of them because I have great gratitude for those who are doing remarkable work online. The different perspectives, the storytelling, all connecting the dots in ways I couldn't have done, these are all responsible for my growth. Here are more than a handful of websites or people that I regularly read that enrich my mind, introduce me to new ideas, trends, and people, and provide a kind of education that is responsible for the work that I am doing and the person I am becoming.

Educational Websites

Brain Pickings (http://www.brainpickings.org): From culture, art, history, psychology, neuroscience, and more, Maria Popova has created a timeless archive of all her learning. A master at dissecting books and unearthing gems of wisdom, you'll find yourself interested in subjects that you weren't aware about.

99u (http://99u.com): This website focuses on empowering creatives. From articles, videos, and an annual live conference, this site has remarkable writers sharing their insight on creativity, psychology, design, management, and more. To get a mere glimpse of what they have to offer, check out their **best of 2013** (99u.com/articles/20648/best-of-2013-top-insights-tips-and-tricks).

Resources

Aeon Magazine (http://aeon.co/magazine/): This site is about nature, culture, and ideas. I love long-form essay reading, so if you're into more in-depth, stimulating reads then this site may be for you. You can check out their most popular essays **here** (http://aeon.co/magazine/most-popular/) to get a glimpse of what the site is about.

TED (http://www.ted.com): Whenever I mention TED people think I'm talking about the movie with the talking teddy bear. The TED conference is where great ideas spread. Speakers from every field imaginable share their ideas, stories, research, understanding, and passion. I've found some of the greatest teachers/heroes on this website alone by using the principles discussed earlier. Their animated videos are one of my favorite educational mediums and can be found on http://ed.ted.com. Watching even one video a day, for 10 to 20 minutes, can instill some insight, curiosity, and interesting discussions.

Medium (http://www.medium.com): This is a blog publishing platform created by the co-founder of Twitter, Evan Williams and Biz Stone. This site covers a multitude of topics from entertainment, cooking, app design, current trends in the marketplace, and a lot more. Though there are many fantastic writers contributing content to the site, an article's popularity is determined by its value rather than who wrote it. I love that. What's even better is that the site is gorgeous. And if you have your own story, you can publish it.

Digital Photography School (http://digital-photography-school.com): This blog is focused entirely on photography — gear, cameras, tips, insights, and more. It has a very interactive community. The creator, Darren Rowse, is a champion blogger. He even runs **Problogger** — a community for aspiring or current bloggers that provides rich insight on blogging — from SEO, design, plug-ins, content creation, marketing, and more.

Big Think (http://bigthink.com): This site is what they call a "knowledge forum." Experts and great thinkers share their insight on a specific topic, say, global warming or big data and how it affects our economy. From Neil deGrasse Tyson to many different university professors to former U.S. president Jimmy Carter, this site is both fascinating and educational.

ASAP Science (https://www.youtube.com/user/AsapSCIENCE): We all have a preferred way of learning a subject. I learn very deeply when I read, but for great retention and understanding it's important to use all your senses. If you're studying a great war, look at maps or watch a documentary to get visuals. If you're learning about an animal, actually look at it while learning about it. I fell in love with animation videos that succinctly teaches a subject or idea. ASAP Science provides concise and informative animation videos on just about everything.

Business/Marketing

Seth Godin (http://sethgodin.typepad.com): Once a day, everyday, for the past 10+ years, Seth Godin has been unleashing wisdom on his blog on subjects like marketing, storytelling, communication, fear, spreading ideas, change, and more. He's an author of over 15 books, all of which are best sellers, and he is my champion. His blog post is the first thing I read every morning. His perspectives on everything from seducing fear to initiative to understanding the marketplace are refreshing, enriching, and worthy of every minute of your time. I had the privilege of being picked for his **3-day seminar**, an event that transformed me (www.motivatedmastery.com/impresario).

Copyblogger (http://www.copyblogger.com): This is by far one of my favorite sites on content marketing, online marketing, writing/blogging

Resources

tips, and anything in between or related. When I was just starting out, I had trouble finding the resources to learn about what I was trying to do. I landed on Copyblogger and it was immensely helpful. They sell software and training but also provide tons of valuable information for free. If you ever thought about publishing a book on Amazon, **I wrote a post for them back in 2012.** (http://www.copyblogger.com/how-to-publish-kindle-ebook/)

Clarity (https://clarity.fm/home): So imagine that you have a problem with your business or maybe the structure of your project is weak. Clarity is a site that creates a bridge between you and an expert in a field. You pay by the minute, get on the phone, ask questions and get answers. Their blog section is also worth reading. I wish I thought of this site/service because it was a problem that I had many years ago.

Harvard Business Review (http://hbr.org): From new and groundbreaking research, HBR offers many different worldviews, great ideas, and rich perspectives from a variety of leaders.

Marie Forleo (http://www.marieforleo.com): Marie is an entrepreneur, best selling author, and runs her website that helps you overcome obstacles both in your business and personal life. She interviews amazing people from all backgrounds and expertise and also shares her own insights. She's brilliant, funny, and it's obvious that her passion and hard work ethic is the building blocks to her successful empire.

Andrew Chen (http://andrewchen.co): Ever wonder what goes on in Silicon Valley? Many of us use the services, apps, and products that are produced there but will never understand what happens behind the scenes. Chen writes essays about startups, tech, marketing, and what goes on in Silicon Valley.

Connect The Dots

Interesting Blogs

Danielle LaPorte (http://www.daniellelaporte.com): Danielle LaPorte is an author, entrepreneur, motivational speaker, and blogger. Her blog and style of writing is something that I've been regularly reading and throughly enjoying. Her perspective on life, career, ambition, business, and desire is unmatched.

Humans Of New York (http://www.humansofnewyork.com): I envy the creator of HONY, Brandon Stanton, and what he has created. He travels around New York City gathering stories and taking portraits. The tales of loss, happiness, failure, change, and heartbreak abound. He asks simple questions like, "What was the saddest moment of your life?" or "If you could give a piece of advice to a crowd, what would you say?" His work is remarkable, and it unfailingly puts you in a position to review your perspective; many times, it humbles you.

Ryan Holiday (http://www.ryanholiday.net): I found Ryan through an interview and his story resonated with me. A college dropout at 19, he apprenticed for Robert Greene and Tucker Max. He's a media strategist, the Marketing Director for American Apparel, and also a best selling author. His blog and his various contributions to many sites contain a great perspective on media, life, publishing, reading, learning, and more. He introduced me to Marcus Aurelius's book *Meditations*, which is my most treasured book.

Zen Habits (http://zenhabits.net): Personal development is one of the most popular niches on the web. Leo Babauta has an amazing story and one of the most popular blogs. His perspective on mindfulness, mediation, living frugally, compassion and more is inspiring. This blog really helped me put my life into perspective when I was going through one of my many slumps.

The Art of Non-Conformity (http://chrisguillebeau.com): Chris is epitome of a nonconformist. He writes about personal development, how to live an unconventional life, travel, and entrepreneurship. He's written two phenomenal books, holds a yearly conference, and is consistently making an impact with the tribe that he's brought together. This is a guy who really empowers you to think differently.

Ramit Sethi (http://www.iwillteachyoutoberich.com): Ramit's advice on personal finance, entrepreneurship, and his use of psychological research to prove his points has helped immensely. His style of writing is what drew me in, but the delivery of his value and promises is what keeps me a loyal reader.

Steven Pressfield (http://www.stevenpressfield.com): Another one of my many great inspirations and heroes, Steven Pressfield is a best selling author of historical fiction and non-fiction. He publishes every Wednesday and his insight is focused on creativity, the Resistance, habits, writing, art, the publishing industry and more. He's one of my favorite writers, and his book, *The War of Art*, is a must-read no matter what you do for a living. It's one of the handful of books that landed on my lap when I was that lost college student, and it profoundly shifted my perspective on life and work.

The Art of Manliness (http://www.artofmanliness.com): This is a fun, informative and obviously male-centric blog. From how to tie a tie to shaving like your grandpa, this blog offers mostly long-form reads on "reviving the lost art of manliness." Even if you don't read this blog, it's interesting to see how a focused topic can amass hundreds of thousands of readers.

Jeff Goins (http://goinswriter.com/about-me/): Jeff is a friend of mine and is also an amazing teacher. His blog is about writing, creativity, change, building a platform, and everything in between — goals, faith, dealing with uncertainty, living mindfully, and more. From his books, online courses, monthly challenges, and free blog updates, it's a great stepping stone to building your engine of knowledge. My favorite part of his blog is the comment section — tons of engagement (usually 100+ comments per post), sharing of stories, insight and more.

James Altucher (http://www.jamesaltucher.com): What can we learn from a guy who lost millions of dollars, made millions, and openly talks about his failures? *Everything*. From quitting your job to self-publishing to reinventing yourself to alternatives routes for college, James Altucher has a unique and fascinating perspective on the topics that ought to be talked about more often. Simply put, he's brilliant and hilarious, and his best selling book *Choose Yourself* is a must-read. He also does a Q&A on Tuesday on his Twitter. You can literally ask him anything — marriage, spiritually, success, money, you name it — and he will help you,

Podcasts/Interviews

The Great Discontent (http://thegreatdiscontent.com): I love interviews because at the core they provide philosophical wisdom about life. The purpose of an interview is to get into the minds of those who are doing interesting and great work. TGD not only has a gorgeous website, but the people they interview provide a chock full of wisdom on life, expertise, how they started, how they recovered from failure,

Resources

transitions in their career, and the elements to their success. You will most certainly discover someone that you can relate to, learn from, and maybe get in contact.

The Good Life Project (http://www.goodlifeproject.com): The Good Life Project provides free videos hosted by Jonathan Fields, a best selling author and entrepreneur. Each episode features an interview with a remarkable individual. It's about genuine, inspiring, educational and vulnerable conversations about how that successful individual built themselves up. Whenever an interview is published, I watch it instantly, usually in the mornings with breakfast. I can't think of a better way to start the day.

Radiolab (http://www.radiolab.org): Their "About" says it better than I ever could: "Radiolab is a show about curiosity. Where sound illuminates ideas, and the boundaries blur between science, philosophy, and human experience." When I first landed on this site, and read those two sentences, I immediately subscribed and started listening to their podcast. It's a simply brilliant site/podcast, a great ally for morning commutes and long sessions on the treadmill.

Unmistakable Creative (http://unmistakablecreative.com): Originally known as BlogcastFM, Srinivas Rao has done us all a favor: He interviews best selling authors, successful entrepreneurs, psychologists, researchers, and artists of all kinds. For about an hour, we get to listen to great questions and receive equally insightful answers. It's impossible to quantify how much I've learned from these interviews, the notes that I've accumulated, and the people I've discovered.

Notes and Further Reading

All books and articles mentioned throughout this book are listed below.

***Letters From a Stoic* by Seneca**: This book has been one of the most influential books that I have ever read. Seneca is a revered Roman stoic philosopher. His perspective on how to live well, philosophy, self-awareness, friendship, stoicism, adversity, and education are profound and relatable to today's tribulations. To get an idea of what this book offers, I wrote about it on my blog: http://motivatedmastery.com/seneca-life-lessons/

***Out of Our Minds* by Sir Ken Robinson:** This book explains and dissects how our education system was created and why. It's rich in history, facts, research, patterns, and goes as far as providing possible solutions to our outdated system. When I read this book, my hatred and demands for traditional education diminished completely.

***Mastery* by Robert Greene:** This book examines the lives of masters, past and present, and debunks the myth of the genius. Mastery is something available to anyone, and the elements that foster mastery are laid out in this book so clearly that it should instill urgency and motivation to start practicing or doing something — and to stop this deluded belief that you aren't capable of doing great things. From Mozart to legendary boxing coach Freddie Roach, Greene provides fascinating research,

Notes and Further Reading

patterns, ideas, and examples to show that living a meaningful life is at the core of what we do and how well we do it.

Steal Like An Artist **by Austin Kleon:** You can read this book in one day and you'll walk away with possibly a new understanding on creativity. You will realize that great art is a combination of other techniques, ideas, and inspiration. You'll learn that most ideas are not original. You'll learn how to steal the right way.

The Icarus Deception **by Seth Godin:** This book focuses on the new economy and what it's built on: art. The old rules are just that, old. We're living in an entirely different world now and it's changing fast. This book doesn't teach you how to play it safe, but rather how to fly higher than ever before. I've read every Seth Godin book and his perspective on everything from marketing, business, and life is refreshing, insightful, and simply *boom*.

Big Questions From Little People and Simple Answers From Great Minds **by Gemma Elwin Harris:** Gather hundreds of questions from elementary school students and have them answered by the greatest minds of our time, and you have this fascinating book. From "Why is the sky blue?" to the very unique and equally insightful question mentioned in this book about Alexander the Great liking frogs, this book is fun, educational, and is a must-read if you're going to have children.

Manage Your Day-to-Day **and** *Maximize Your Potential* **by Jocelyn K. Glei, a 99u series:** Two gems that, if devoured slowly and with care, will most likely motivate you to start working smarter, take risks, and expand your perspective on what makes a fruitful career. *Manage Your Day-to-Day* is about productivity and working smarter. They get experts from a variety of fields to share their insight and understanding of what it means to be truly productive, live mindfully, and live in the present. *Maximize Your Potential* is about risk taking, initiative, and building an incredible career. Both books are concise but deeply impactful. The amount of notes and research from these two books supplemented my commonplace book greatly.

Happy Birthday, Brain Pickings: 7 Things I Learned In 7 Years of Reading, Writing, and Living by Maria Popova (http://www.brainpickings.org/index.php/2013/10/23/7-lessons-from-7-years/): Maria Popova is one of my great inspirations when it comes to writing, creating, building a valuable and educational platform, and learning. I am deeply inspired by those who do great work, and I always wonder what goes on inside their heads. What do they think about? What are their principles? How do they do what they do? This piece is fantastic and timeless.

How and Why to Keep a "Commonplace Book" by Ryan Holiday (http://thoughtcatalog.com/ryan-holiday/2013/08/how-and-why-to-keep-a-commonplace-book/): I started building a commonplace book early when I started to voraciously read because I knew taking copious notes would somehow benefit me in my later endeavors. When I landed on this article, it provided a deeper appreciation of this tool and a unique perspective. Out of all the tools available in your didactic pursuits, this is by far the most rewarding and helpful. I will go as far as saying that you should immediately utilize this tool when you finish this book and pick up another one.

Project Gutenberg (http://www.gutenberg.org): This site has over 42,000 *free* eBooks in a variety of formats, i.e., a Kindle book or ePub format. It's priceless. You can find a lot of classics — and, in my experience, it's usually the classics that contain a great deal of commonplace book material.

Krypton Community College (http://sethgodin.typepad.com/krypton_community_college/): Although it's solely our responsibility to enrich our minds and to evolve our understanding on the subjects that are part of our daily lives, it's vital that we engage in other forms of learning: group learning. Indeed, researchers work together, as do organizations, movements, businesses, and more. This book wasn't a solo effort, neither are the apps or products that you use. The one glaring problem that I found in traditional education was that the professors love hearing themselves talk. Speaking for myself, I find great joy and reward in learning when engaging in meaningful discussions. Seth Godin has gathered a bunch of interns and created Krypton Community College. It's where you can find local like-minded individuals to come together to learn and share ideas. There are lesson plans divided into weeks, questions to ask, objectives to accomplish, and more. There's an outline for both students and organizer. There are no excuses to not use this free service.

Acknowledgements

To be read is a great privilege, but to be read and also change minds? It's the deepest feeling of gratitude a writer can ever have.

To my editors, Nils Parker and Ann Maynard: Out of the 3 books that I've written, this was the first book edited by real pros, and wow, what a difference indeed. The feedback and guidance has helped me connect new dots to further improve my writing. The editing was meticulous, thoughtful, and at times, I sat there deeply thinking about how or why you changed a specific line. Reviewing your work was an educational experience in itself. You turned a dull stone into a flawless gem.

To my designer, Laura Sly: The fact that I don't ever have to change designers saves me a lot of time and stress. But the fact that you're excellent at what you do — and getting better at a pace that is unfathomable — is what gives me confidence and hope. Your dedication, passion, and creativity inspire me daily.

To my friends who put up with my rants, doubts, brainstorming sessions, and insecurities: Dinner on me.

To my heroes: Thank you for the work that you're doing. Thank you for showing me how to connect the dots and why it's so important

Acknowledgements

to do it on a daily basis. Thank you for inspiring me with your work ethic, virtues, and passion. I would not be who I am if it weren't for you generously sharing the dots that you've connected throughout your lives.

Places you can find me:

My blog: http://www.motivatedmastery.com

Twitter: @Pauljun_

Facebook: facebook.com/motivatedmastery

Made in the USA
Lexington, KY
06 December 2017